**Blastoff! Readers** are carefully developed by literacy experts to build reading stamina and move students toward fluency by combining standards-based content with developmentally appropriate text.

 **Level 1** provides the most support through repetition of high-frequency words, light text, predictable sentence patterns, and strong visual support.

 **Level 2** offers early readers a bit more challenge through varied sentences, increased text load, and text-supportive special features.

 **Level 3** advances early-fluent readers toward fluency through increased text load, less reliance on photos, advancing concepts, longer sentences, and more complex special features.

★ **Blastoff! Universe**

  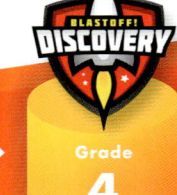

Reading Level: Grade K → Grades 1–3 → Grade 4

This edition first published in 2024 by Bellwether Media, Inc.

No part of this publication may be reproduced in whole or in part without written permission of the publisher. For information regarding permission, write to Bellwether Media, Inc., Attention: Permissions Department, 6012 Blue Circle Drive, Minnetonka, MN 55343.

Library of Congress Cataloging-in-Publication Data

Names: Davies, Monika, author.
Title: Greece / by Monika Davies.
Description: Minneapolis, MN : Bellwether Media, Inc., 2024. | Series: Blastoff! Readers: Countries of the World | Includes bibliographical references and index. | Audience: Ages 5-8 | Audience: Grades 2-3 | Summary: "Relevant images match informative text in this introduction to Greece. Intended for students in kindergarten through third grade"– Provided by publisher.
Identifiers: LCCN 2023046588 (print) | LCCN 2023046589 (ebook) | ISBN 9798886877946 (library binding) | ISBN 9798886878882 (ebook)
Subjects: LCSH: Greece–Juvenile literature.
Classification: LCC DF717 .D38 2024 (print) | LCC DF717 (ebook) | DDC 914.9504–dc23/eng/20231012
LC record available at https://lccn.loc.gov/2023046588
LC ebook record available at https://lccn.loc.gov/2023046589

Text copyright © 2024 by Bellwether Media, Inc. BLASTOFF! READERS and associated logos are trademarks and/or registered trademarks of Bellwether Media, Inc.

Editor: Rachael Barnes   Series Design: Gabriel Hilger   Book Designer: Kathleen Petelinsek
Printed in the United States of America, North Mankato, MN.

Table of Contents

All About Greece	4
Land and Animals	6
Life in Greece	12
Greece Facts	20
Glossary	22
To Learn More	23
Index	24

All About Greece

Athens

Greece is a country in southern Europe. The nation's capital is Athens.

Greece has a long history of art and science. Many people visit the country's **ancient** sites.

Land and Animals

Greece has thousands of hilly islands. Seas surround them.

Mountains stand tall across most of the mainland. Forests cover them. **Plains** fill the lower areas.

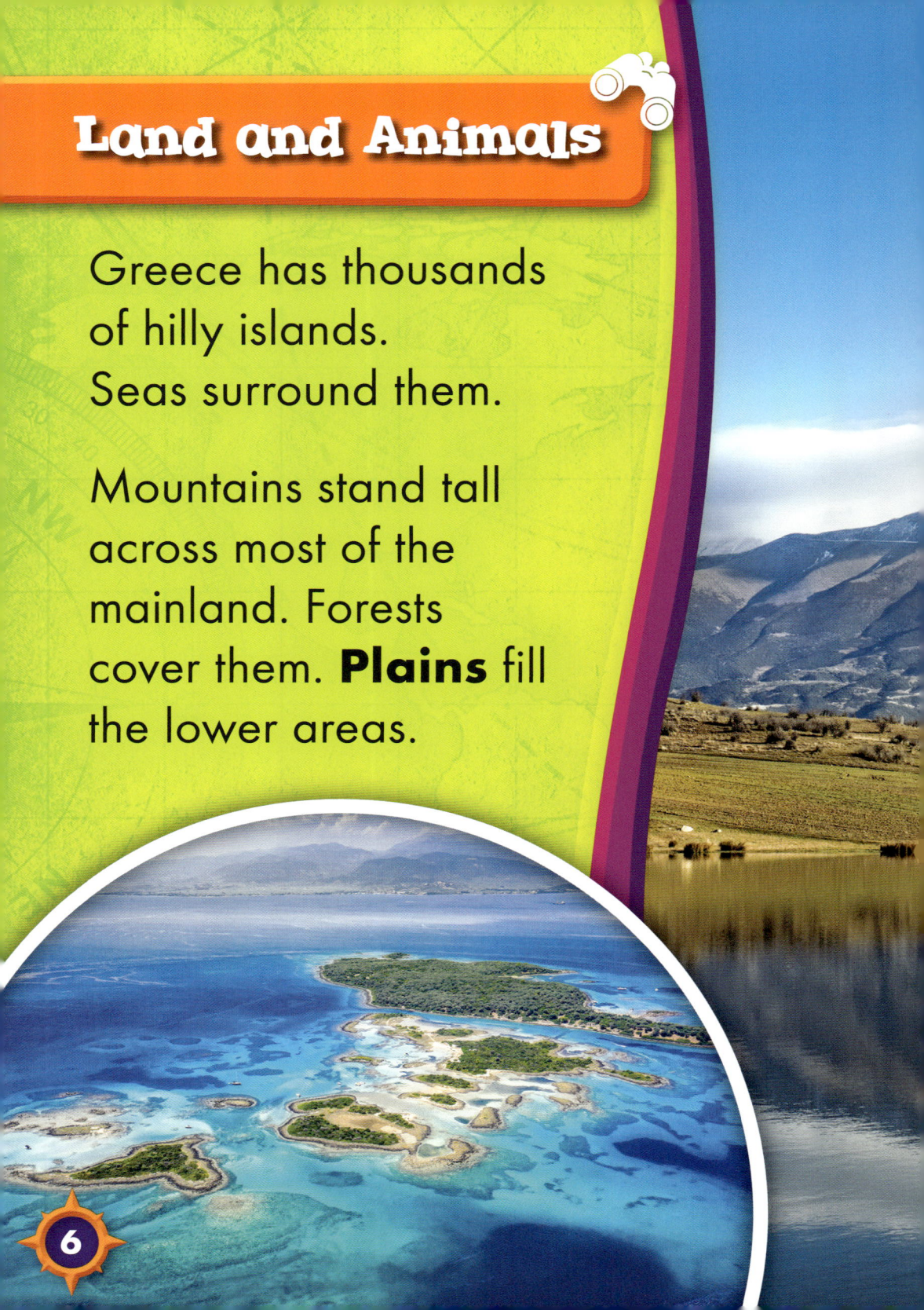

Mount Olympus

Size: around 9,570 feet (2,917 meters) tall

Famous For: Greece's tallest mountain

Summers in Greece are sunny and dry. Winters are mild and wet. Snow falls in the mountains.

Earthquakes are common all year.

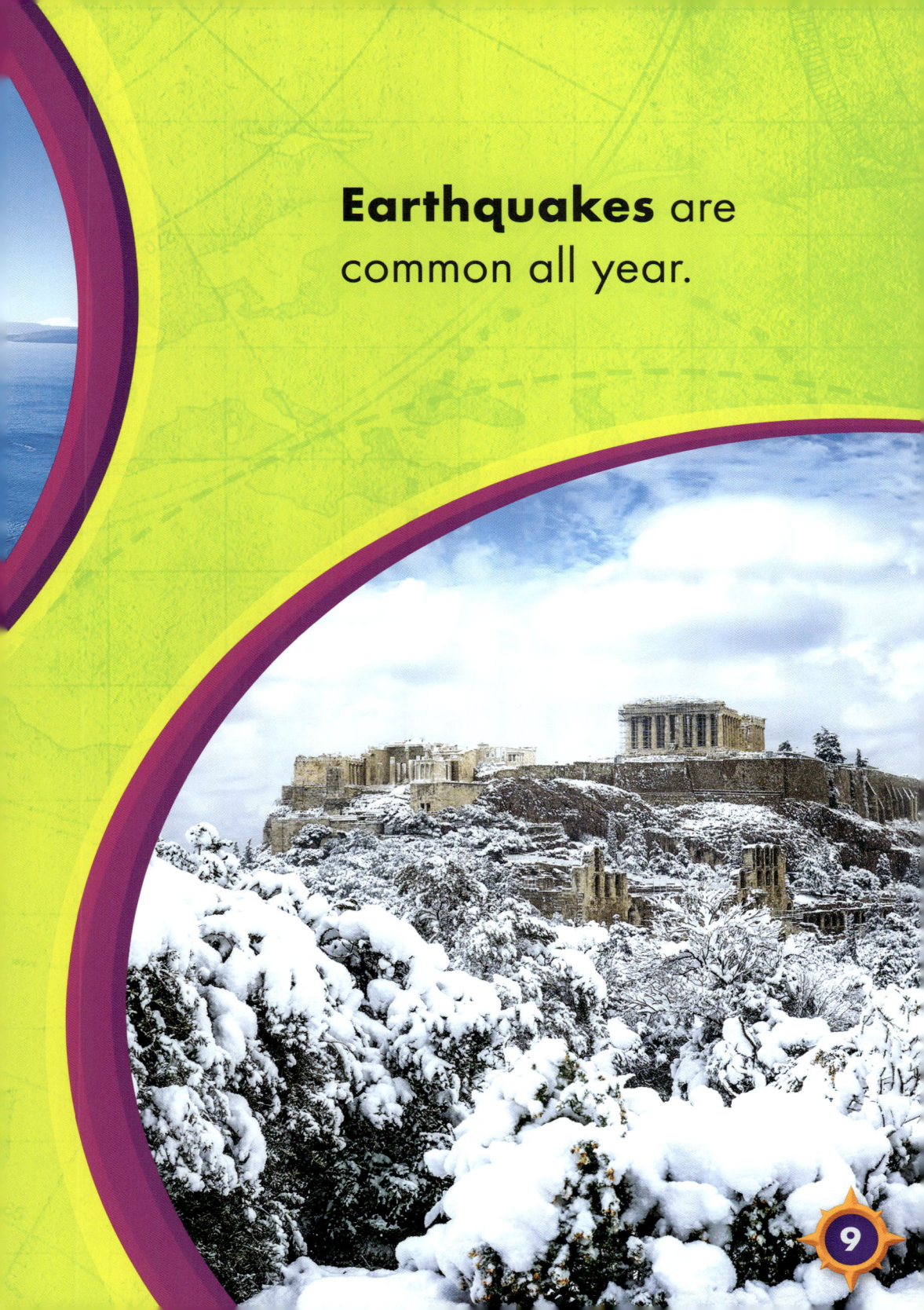

Martens and brown bears live in forests. Little owls fly overhead.

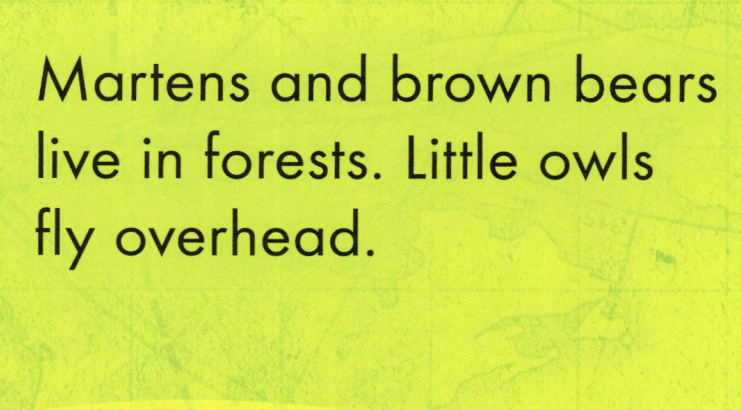
brown bears

Animals of Greece

beech marten

little owl

European hare

blackspot sea bream

Hares hop on grassy hills.
Sea breams swim in the seas.

Life in Greece

Nearly all Greeks speak Greek. They often have a Greek background. Most belong to the **Greek Orthodox** Church.

Many people live in seaside cities. Athens is the largest.

Greek Orthodox Church

soccer

basketball

Family is important to Greeks. People eat large meals with their **extended families**.

Greeks also play soccer and basketball. Many go to the theater.

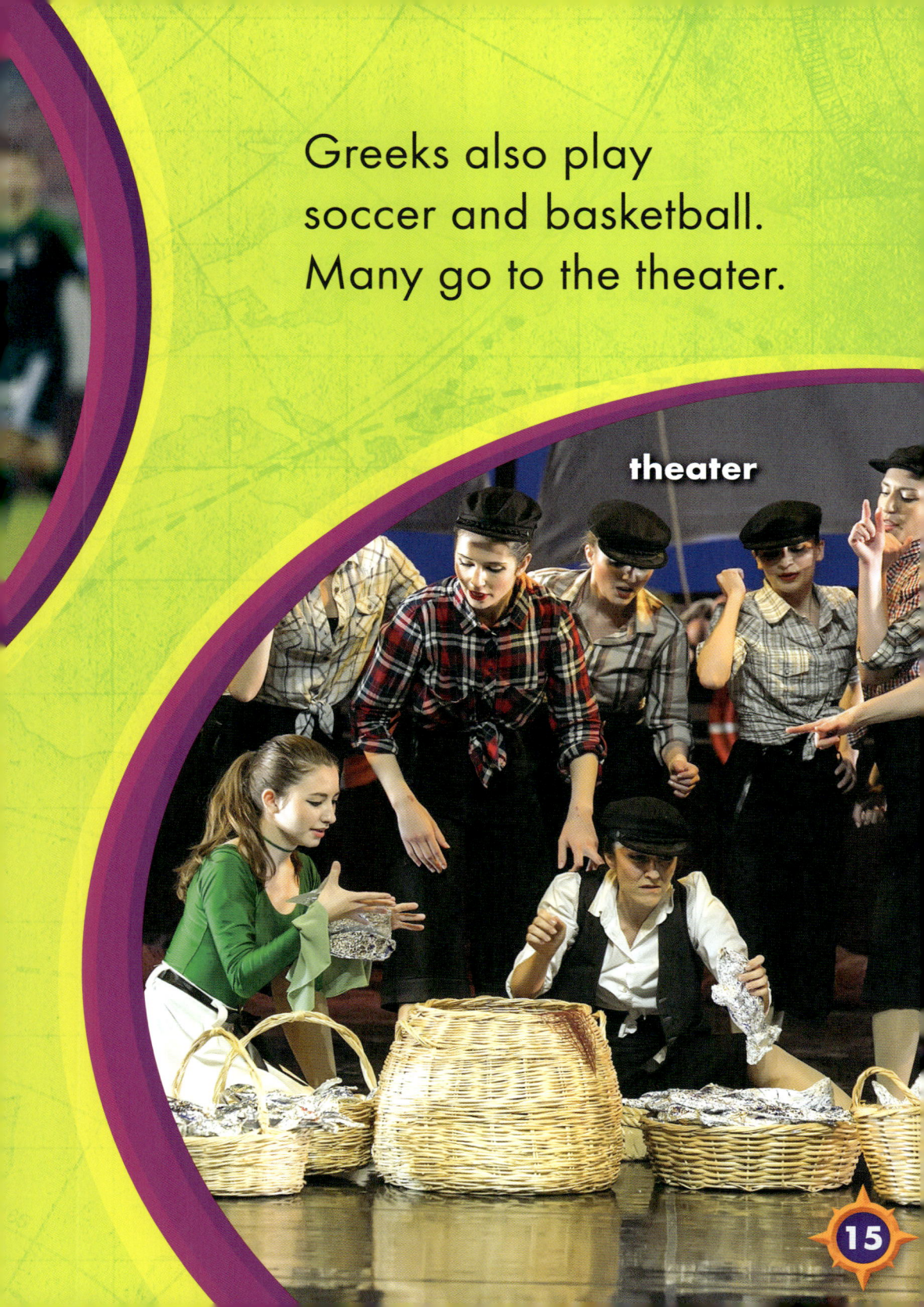

theater

Olives and olive oil are paired with most Greek meals. *Moussaka* is a baked lamb and eggplant dish.

Greek Foods

olives and olive oil

moussaka

tzatziki

baklava

olives

Tzatziki is a yogurt and cucumber dip. Baklava is a sweet treat!

Independence Day

Greece's national holiday is Independence Day. There are big parades.

Greeks also **celebrate** Easter. People attend church. They eat large meals. Family gatherings are a joyful part of Greek life!

Greece Facts

Size:
50,949 square miles
(131,957 square kilometers)

Population:
10,497,595 (2023)

National Holiday:
Independence Day (March 25)

Main Language:
Greek

Capital City:
Athens

Famous Face

Name: Giannis Antetokounmpo

Famous For: basketball player

Religions

- Greek Orthodox 85%
- Muslim 2%
- none 9%
- other 4%

Top Landmarks

Acropolis of Athens

Delphi

Palace of Knossos

Glossary

ancient—from long ago

celebrate—to do something special or fun for an event, occasion, or holiday

earthquakes—sudden movements of the earth's crust

extended families—family groups that include parents, children, grandparents, aunts, and uncles

Greek Orthodox—relating to the Orthodox Church of Greece; Orthodox is a type of Christianity common in Eastern Europe, especially Greece and Russia.

plains—large areas of flat land

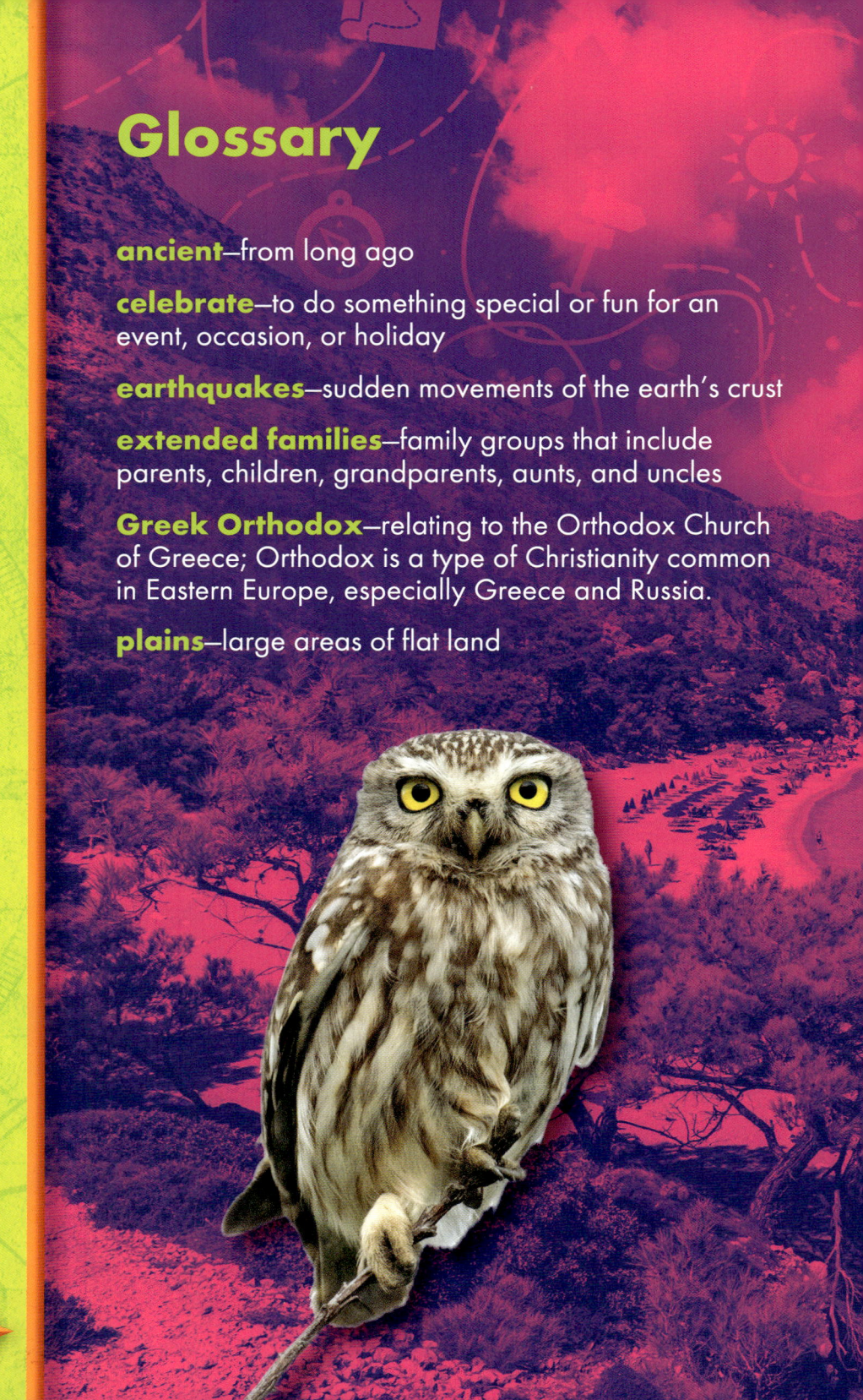

To Learn More

AT THE LIBRARY

Spanier, Kristine. *Parthenon*. Minneapolis, Minn.: Jump!, 2021.

Tabachnik, Anna T. *Greece*. New York, N.Y.: Scholastic, 2019.

Vallepur, Shalini. *People Did What in Ancient Greece?* New York, N.Y.: Crabtree Publishing Company, 2020.

ON THE WEB

FACTSURFER

Factsurfer.com gives you a safe, fun way to find more information.

1. Go to www.factsurfer.com.
2. Enter "Greece" into the search box and click 🔍.
3. Select your book cover to see a list of related content.

Index

animals, 10, 11
art, 5
Athens, 4, 5, 12
basketball, 14, 15
capital (see Athens)
cities, 12
earthquakes, 9
Easter, 19
Europe, 4
food, 16, 17
forests, 6, 10
Greece facts, 20–21
Greek, 12, 13
Greek Orthodox Church, 12, 19
Independence Day, 18
islands, 6
map, 5
Mount Olympus, 7

mountains, 6, 7, 8
people, 5, 12, 14, 15, 19
plains, 6
say hello, 13
science, 5
seas, 6, 11, 12
sites, 5
snow, 8
soccer, 14, 15
summers, 8
theater, 15
winters, 8

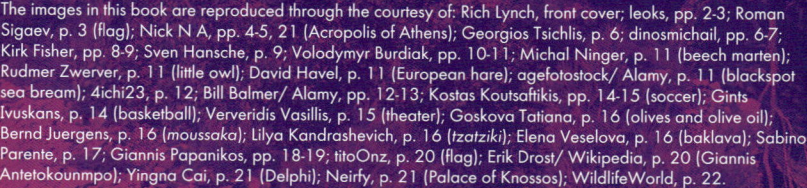

The images in this book are reproduced through the courtesy of: Rich Lynch, front cover; leoks, pp. 2-3; Roman Sigaev, p. 3 (flag); Nick N A, pp. 4-5, 21 (Acropolis of Athens); Georgios Tsichlis, p. 6; dinosmichail, pp. 6-7; Kirk Fisher, pp. 8-9; Sven Hansche, p. 9; Volodymyr Burdiak, pp. 10-11; Michal Ninger, p. 11 (beech marten); Rudmer Zwerver, p. 11 (little owl); David Havel, p. 11 (European hare); agefotostock/ Alamy, p. 11 (blackspot sea bream); 4ichi23, p. 12; Bill Balmer/ Alamy, pp. 12-13; Kostas Koutsaftikis, pp. 14-15 (soccer); Gints Ivuskans, p. 14 (basketball); Ververidis Vasillis, p. 15 (theater); Goskova Tatiana, p. 16 (olives and olive oil); Bernd Juergens, p. 16 (*moussaka*); Lilya Kandrashevich, p. 16 (*tzatziki*); Elena Veselova, p. 16 (baklava); Sabino Parente, p. 17; Giannis Papanikos, pp. 18-19; titoOnz, p. 20 (flag); Erik Drost/ Wikipedia, p. 20 (Giannis Antetokounmpo); Yingna Cai, p. 21 (Delphi); Neirfy, p. 21 (Palace of Knossos); WildlifeWorld, p. 22.